Original title:
Rooted in Love

Copyright © 2025 Creative Arts Management OÜ
All rights reserved.

Author: Amelia Montgomery
ISBN HARDBACK: 978-1-80581-811-3
ISBN PAPERBACK: 978-1-80581-338-5
ISBN EBOOK: 978-1-80581-811-3

Where Love Takes Hold

In a garden of giggles, we grow,
With our quirks as seeds, to and fro.
You steal my fries, I snatch your drink,
In this circus of love, we never sink.

Dancing around in mismatched socks,
Building our dreams like Jenga blocks.
We laugh at the mess, we roll on the floor,
Together we're silly, who could want more?

Grounded Together

Two peas in a pod, so tightly bound,
We laugh like kids, no worries around.
You trip on your words, I trip on my feet,
In this slapstick dance, we can't be beat.

Like a mismatched pair of shoes we are,
Wobbling through life but always ajar.
With you by my side, chaos feels right,
Each blunder a joy, a hilarious sight.

The Tapestry of Us

With threads of laughter, we weave our tale,
Each stitch a chuckle, we cannot fail.
You joke about aliens, I snort soda pop,
In this fabric of fun, we'll never stop.

We pick colors bright, even when they clash,
In our tapestry, no moments feel brash.
Every silly bicker, a patch we adore,
Together we've made, a love that can soar.

A Floral Symphony

In a bouquet of chaos, we bloom wide,
Sunflowers sway to the beat, oh with pride.
You hum off-key, I dance out of tune,
Together we spark like a sunlit afternoon.

Petals of laughter, fragrance of fun,
In our garden of mishaps, we've already won.
Bees buzzing by, join our playful song,
In this floral symphony, we both belong.

A Symphony of Hearts

In the garden of giggles, we dance and we sway,
Your laughter's the melody that brightens my day.
Potted in friendship, with roots oh so tight,
We croon silly songs under the moonlight.

With bouquets of puns, our weeds turn to gold,
We twirl through the troubles like stories retold.
Each joke is a tulip, each pun is a vine,
Together we blossom, oh how we entwine!

Heartfelt Tendrils

You sprout silly sentiments like flowers in spring,
I'm struck by your quirks, oh the joy that you bring!
Tendrils of laughter wrap round every slight,
In this comedy garden, we're a festive sight.

Like twinkling tomatoes, we pop beyond measure,
With root beer floats we celebrate our treasure.
Our hearts are like cabbages, layered and sweet,
In the patch of affection, there's never defeat.

The Clay of Togetherness

With hands in the clay, we shape what we see,
Creating a pot of pure glee, can't you see?
A pinch of your wit, a dash of my charm,
Together we mold our humorous farm.

As we knead through the chaos with laughter and fun,
Our masterpiece grows under the bright, sunny sun.
In this quirky workshop of playful delight,
We sculpt our own story, it's a comical sight.

The Depth of Our Bond

Like deep-rooted laughter that echoes through time,
Our friendship grows stronger, like lemon and lime.
With each little chuckle, our hearts intertwine,
In the comedy club of life, we always shine.

We dive deep for giggles, swim wide for some cheer,
In the ocean of friendship, there's nothing to fear.
With quirks in abundance, we float without care,
Building boats of joy, sailing the laughter-air.

Timeless Connection

In a dance of socks and mismatched shoes,
We trip on laughs, not fears or blues.
Two hearts collide in a tangle of jest,
Who knew love's chaos could be the best?

With your quirky smile like a zany pie,
You make mundane moments soar and fly.
We share our quirks, our laughter so bright,
Like beacons in the dark of the night.

Over burnt toast and coffee that's cold,
We find our treasures, more precious than gold.
Your silly faces bring joy to my heart,
Without a doubt, we were made to be part.

So let's toast to the craziness we share,
In a world of laughter, there's always a pair.
Through every riddle and raucous delight,
Our timeless connection glimmers so bright.

The Heart's Sanctuary

In our sanctuary filled with quirky art,
A treasure trove made just for two hearts.
Your terrible jokes, they make me crack up,
Like a soda can that just won't shut up!

When you steal my fries, don't think I won't fight,
But sweet ketchup hugs make it all feel right.
In the starlit garden, we dance in delight,
Laughing at shadows until the daylight.

With your goofy dance moves and your playful cheer,
You chase away any lingering fear.
A symphony of chuckles, our private show,
In the theater of love, we steal the glow.

So here's to the clumsiness, the joy we embrace,
Creating memories in this funny space.
Our hearts intertwine in a playful spree,
In this quirky haven, just you and me.

In Everlasting Circles

In circles round, we chase our tails,
Like puppies lost in playful trails.
With every spin, we share a laugh,
In this sweet dance, we have our path.

Your goofy grin, my heart's delight,
In coffee spills and late-night bites.
We stumble through, like shoes untied,
With love's embrace, we cannot hide.

The Tapestry of Us

Woven threads of silly schemes,
Like tangled hair and wild dreams.
We stitch our days with laughter's thread,
In every hug, snorts punctuate our bed.

Your quirks, my fuel, my heart's delight,
In scrambled words, we find our light.
Each silly joke, a lasting thread,
In this wild weave, we forge ahead.

Deeply Bound

In shoelaces tied, we find our way,
Through twisted paths, we laugh and play.
With every step, a comedy,
Our hearts beat wild, a melody.

Like socks that vanish in the wash,
We search for love, a jovial posh.
In goofy moments, we are found,
Two hearts aligned, forever bound.

Whispered Affections

In whispers shared, our secrets grow,
Like hidden snacks, we both know.
With silly voices, we make our way,
In the chaos, we laugh and play.

Your side-eye glances make me grin,
In every twist, our joy begins.
With quirky tales, our bond's defined,
In whispered jests, our hearts entwined.

The Embrace of Time

In a world where socks go to hide,
We stay tangled, side by side.
Like coffee stains on a bank receipt,
Our quirks make life so sweet.

Time ticks slow on our kitchen clock,
We dance to the rhythm of a clock's tick-tock.
With laughter echoing off the walls,
We let our love bounce and fall.

Echoes of Commitment

Like the echo of a snoring cat,
Love finds all the cozy spots to splat.
Through mismatched socks and lost keys,
We navigate life with such ease.

Every promise whispered at night,
Is signed in coffee and hugs so tight.
In flip-flops or boots, we roam free,
With laughter echoing endlessly.

Harmony in Bloom

Like daffodils growing in a shoe,
Our love blooms in places quite askew.
In the garden of laughter, we plant our seeds,
With giggles and quirks, fulfilling our needs.

We prune the thorns with jovial jokes,
Amidst the chaos, our hearts invoke.
The bees may buzz, but we don't mind,
In our floral chaos, love is kind.

With Every Thorn, a Rose

Life can sting like a bee on the run,
But in the chaos, we find our fun.
With every thorn that jabs our toes,
We harvest laughter that just grows.

Through balmy nights and clumsy falls,
We turn our stumbles into calls.
For even pricks can bring a cheer,
In this quirky romance we hold dear.

Ties That Bind

In a garden where weeds play pranks,
My grandma's advice fills the empty flanks.
"Love's like a rope that won't let you fall,
Unless it's a prank—then just take the call!"

Neighbors march in their matching slippers,
Debating the best way to plant odd zippers.
Grandpa chuckles as he lights his pipe,
"The best love's got style, and a sense of hype!"

Deep Within the Heart

Beneath the fluff of a doughnut hole,
Lies a love that tickles, oh what a goal!
It juggles emotions like a clumsy clown,
Making smiles bloom, never a frown.

So, let's build a fort with warm fuzzy thoughts,
Dodge sad moments like they're bad shots.
With bits of laughter, we'll draw the line,
In this crazy game, we've all got time!

Whispers of Affection

In a café where spoons start to dance,
Love whispers softly, sparking romance.
"Can I borrow your fries?" a bold claim,
Love's just a burger, with a side of fame!

Between sips of coffee and cakes that gleam,
We spot a cat plotting her grand scheme.
"Love is like magic," she purrs with a stare,
"Just sprinkle some laughter—there's enough to share!"

Where the Wildflowers Grow

In a field where the daisies wear funny hats,
Lovers skitter like nervous bats.
With silly dances and goofy grins,
Their hearts beat wildly, every time it spins.

Butterflies giggle as they flit about,
"Love's a bouquet!" they sing out loud.
So let's prance through life, like wildflowers do,
With laughter as sunshine, so fresh and so true!

Beneath the Canopy

Under the trees where squirrels play,
We argue about which way's the best way.
You say left, I say right, oh what a mess,
Yet here we are, still feeling blessed.

With branches that sway, we dance in the breeze,
You steal my shade, but I steal your cheese.
Laughter echoes, our roots intertwine,
In this goofy grove, it's just you and I.

Stems of Connection

Like vines that twist and creep all around,
You climbed my heart, but I tripped and fell down.
Tangled together, we giggle and cheer,
Your puns are the blooms, they grow year by year.

With stems that wobble, we reach for the sun,
You soak my soul, now isn't that fun?
In the garden of jest, where laughter is key,
We're two silly plants, wild and free.

Growing Together

In a pot too small, we both have a fit,
You squish my side, but it's all worth the wit.
Watered by jokes, we sprout taller each day,
Competing for light in our quirky ballet.

With roots in the dirt, we find plenty to chew,
Planting our dreams, like daisies askew.
Together we flourish, a hilarious show,
Watch our antics grow, and oh how they glow!

Love's Fertile Ground

In the soil we share, we dig for delight,
You wear my hat, and I just might bite!
Our laughter's the fertilizer, bright and bold,
Watch our garden blossom, a sight to behold.

With weeds of mishaps, we pull side by side,
Your goofy faces I just can't abide!
Yet still, I cherish each hilarious fight,
In this patch of joy, it all feels so right.

Embracing the Unseen

In the garden of hearts, we dance with glee,
With weeds wearing hats, as quirky as can be.
A dandelion's wish, a ladybug's grin,
Each laugh is a treasure, let the giggles begin!

With invisible strings, we twirl and we sway,
A blindfolded race where we all lose our way.
Chasing after shadows that tease and that play,
Hand in hand we tumble, 'til the sun goes away.

From Earth to Embrace

A potato in slippers, it rolls with delight,
Whispering tales of its vegetable plight.
Carrots dressed in tuxedos, they all stand in line,
Offering punch and a bottle of brine!

In dirt we find humor, in mud there's a song,
The worms are the DJs, and the roots hum along.
Each tickle from beetles ignites the good cheer,
In the soil of silliness, we hold our dear friends near.

In the Shade of Affection

Beneath leafy canopies, giggles abound,
Where squirrels wear glasses and chatter around.
A hug from a tree is the silliest prize,
With branches that tickle and don't mind the skies.

The bumblebees buzz with a rhythm so sweet,
In a polka dance-off, they can't admit defeat.
As flowers keep blushing, enamored and bright,
We twirl in the shadows, embracing the light.

The Essence of Belonging

In a pot of confusion, we stir with a grin,
Mixing up flavors like goats on a whim.
Spaghetti on Tuesdays, tacos on more,
Each bite brings us laughter, the heart's open door.

The chaos is comfy, a jumbled embrace,
With socks all mismatched, we dance at our pace.
Like pizza with pickles or ice cream in stew,
The essence of friendship is silly and true.

Threads of Solace

In the garden where gnomes dance,
Threads of laughter weave in chance.
Flowers chuckle, petals sway,
Tickled by the sun's bright ray.

Squirrels sharing secret treats,
Bumblebees in tiny feats.
Every twig, a joke to tell,
Nature's humor rings so well.

Whispers in the Roots

Tree trunks gossip, roots confide,
Worms and beetles join the ride.
Fungi giggle at their jokes,
Sprouting smiles in leafy cloaks.

Rabbits laugh at all the fuss,
As the wind starts to discuss.
Underneath, a world so sly,
Nature's antics, oh my, oh my!

Harmonized by Nature

Crickets play a nightly tune,
Underneath a silver moon.
Fireflies dance with glimmering grace,
Nature's band, a funny place!

Ducks quack rhymes, the frogs keep beat,
Even the mud jumps to its feet.
In this ruckus, joy unfolds,
Laughter in the air, so bold!

Beneath the Surface

Under grass, where ants conspire,
Nibbles turn to wild desire.
Mole chefs whip up dirt delight,
As they plot their underground night.

Earthworms dream of pizza pies,
While sleepy roots exchange surprise.
With every wriggle, laugh, and cheer,
A world of giggles down here, oh dear!

The Heart's Foundation

In a garden of giggles, seeds were sown,
Where love grows tall and quite overgrown.
A tomato's blush as sweet as pie,
Said, 'I'm the reason bananas cry!'

When daisies dance in the summer light,
Tulips tease with their colors so bright.
But a daffodil shouted in chains of green,
'You won't squash my dreams, you veggie machine!'

Tethers of the Heart

From kite strings tangled in wind's warm embrace,
To love's little quirks that often misplace.
A rubber band holds tight with a snap,
As two hearts collide like a clap of a flap!

Two socks mismatched, their colors collide,
Yet they waltz through laundry, love's joyful ride.
One's striped, the other's polka-dot flair,
Together, they're chaos, but oh! What a pair!

From Petals to Promises

With petals as confetti, we danced in bloom,
Silly bees buzzing, making quite a room.
A flower swayed, wearing laughter like lace,
While a stubborn weed joined the happy race!

Promises whispered in the soft summer air,
Like fireflies winking, without a care.
A sunflower grinned, its face to the sky,
Mimicking smiles that could make clouds fly!

Evergreen Affection

In a forest of chuckles, trees grew so wide,
Their branches told tales with the birds as their guide.
A pine swayed softly, its needles said, 'Hey!'
While a cheeky sapling danced in pure play!

Beneath a green canopy, shadows would tease,
As the leaves whispered secrets carried by breeze.
But the roots kept on giggling, a wise, silly bunch,
Saying love grows deeper than the wildest punch!

Bonded by Dreams

In a world where socks sometimes roam,
We find our way back to feel like home.
Chasing butterflies, or so we claim,
With pancakes on Sunday, we play our game.

Through silly dances and midnight calls,
We laugh at the shadows that bounce on the walls.
Whispering secrets under the stars,
In our silly kingdom, we're both rockstars.

Maps drawn on napkins, our plans on the fly,
Eating ice cream while wondering why.
The universe winks with every shared laugh,
Life's but a circus, and we are the half.

So here's to our journey, a marvelous scheme,
Crafted in giggles, and stitched with a dream.
Hand in hand, through mischief we glide,
A partnership blooming, can't let it hide.

In the Embrace of Time

Tick-tock goes the clock, what a bizarre tune,
We dance like clockwork to the light of the moon.
With each silly moment and zany delight,
We spin through the chaos, from day into night.

We juggle our worries, toss them in air,
Like juggling clowns, we've not a care.
With pizza on Friday and movies on Sunday,
Every moment with you is always 'yay!' and 'hurray!'

Time is the prankster, pulling our strings,
Yet here, side by side, we're the queens and kings.
Measured in laughter, not minutes or hours,
Our hearts bloom like wild, unchained flowers.

Through all of the moments you lend me your hand,
With each silly footprint we draw in the sand.
So let's build our castle, both quirky and sweet,
In the embrace of time, oh how life feels complete!

Tangled in Devotion

In a web of laughs and hilarious bumbles,
We find joy even when life stumbles.
With tangled socks and mismatched shoes,
In our circus of love, we'll never lose.

Wrapped up in chaos, oh what a treat,
We dance through the kitchen, with two left feet.
Spinning like tops, our laughter a roar,
Who knew that chores could be such a chore?

With peanut butter stories and jellybean dreams,
We weave our reality in whimsical themes.
Every misstep, a new dance of surprise,
In our tangled devotion, true fun never dies.

Through the storms that may come, or the sunshine we see,
This jumbled adventure is perfect for me.
So here's to our quirks, both wild and the plain,
Embracing the nonsense is our sweetest gain.

A Sturdy Foundation

In a house built of giggles, where humor does bloom,
We craft our adventures and banish the gloom.
With pillows for walls and blankets for roofs,
Every day's treasure is counted in goofs.

Like a strong cup of coffee, our bond gives us cheer,
Spilling laughter like sugary soda, oh dear!
When life throws us lemons, we bake up a pie,
With sprinkles of joy, we give it a try.

We measure our moments with tickles and grins,
Creating our legacy where laughter begins.
With a sturdy foundation, we dance through the night,
In a castle of joy where everything's right.

Here's to the laughter, our wild serenade,
In this quirky creation, together we wade.
So pass me the cookies, let's savor the fun,
With a wink and a smile, our journey's begun!

The Essence of Belonging

In a world of odd socks, we find our way,
Dancing in circles where giggles play.
With mismatched spoons and silly hats,
We raise our cups, 'Cheers!' to the chitchats!

Laughter spills like coffee stains,
We gather close, forget the pains.
In quirky hugs and playful jests,
Together we're perfect, no need for tests.

Wandering thoughts on a whimsical breeze,
Like dandelions swaying with ease.
Each tickle of joy, a thread in our seam,
We stitch our dreams with a thread of cream.

So here's to the chaos, the mess and the fun,
In a tapestry woven, we're all just one.
With hearts wide open, we color outside,
In this joyful circus, we take in our stride.

Flourish Without Fear

In gardens where laughter blooms so bright,
We wiggle like worms and dance with delight.
With sun hats askew and joy on our sleeves,
We giggle and twist like whimsical leaves.

Sprouting ideas, we're never too shy,
Like veggies on stilts, we reach for the sky.
A carrot in clogs, a tomato in gowns,
Together we flourish, destroying our frowns.

With bees buzzing tunes, and frogs crooning songs,
In this vibrant patch, nothing feels wrong.
We share our quirkiness, nutty and real,
In laughter's embrace, we learn how to heal.

So jump in the dirt, embrace all the fun,
As plants of the earth, we shine like the sun.
With roots intertwined, we're a riotous cheer,
In the garden of life, we'll flourish, my dear!

A Haven of Hearts

In the shelter of friendship, we play hide and seek,
With laughter as echoes, it's joy that we speak.
Silly secret codes, like owls in the night,
In a fortress of giggles, we take our flight.

With blankets of love that wrap us so tight,
We build forts of dreams in the soft moonlight.
Whipped cream on noses and cake on our hats,
We dance through the mess like two playful cats.

In a galaxy filled with tinfoil stars,
We roam through the cosmos and giggle at jars.
Capturing wishes, we're silly and free,
In this haven of hearts, just you and me.

So let's paint the sky with colors so bold,
With laughter like sunshine, our stories unfold.
We'll sprinkle the world with glitter and cheer,
In this haven of hearts, we'll always be near.

Joined at the Roots

Like two tangled vines, we sway and we twirl,
With laughter that bubbles, we give it a whirl.
In the shade of our jokes, we take a quick nap,
Dreaming of adventures on a whimsical map.

With silly handshakes and high-fiving trees,
We dance on the breezes, our worries at ease.
Through storms and bright sunshine, our branches entwine,
In this garden of chaos, your heart beats with mine.

We share our odd quirks, like socks with no mates,
In the tapestry woven of whimsical fates.
From roots deeply sown, our laughter takes flight,
In a world full of colors, where everything's bright.

So here's to our growth, a fumble and cheer,
In this jungle of life, there's nothing to fear.
With hearts that are goofy, we'll always stand tall,
Joined at the roots, we're having a ball!

The Soil of Togetherness

In the garden of our quirks, we bloom,
With laughter loud, we chase away gloom.
Your socks on the floor, my hair on the sink,
Together we're a mess, but we hardly think.

We plant inside jokes and water with glee,
Sometimes you giggle, sometimes it's me.
Yet, in our chaos, love's sweet refrain,
Makes weeding through life a delightful gain.

Our roots are silly, our flowers askew,
With you by my side, there's nothing we rue.
Let's dance in the dirt, ignore what they say,
For in this wild patch, we find our way.

So cheers to the moments, both silly and grand,
With every small blunder, we're hand in hand.
In the soil of togetherness, let's spread our cheer,
For in this odd garden, there's nothing to fear.

Entwined Souls

You roll your eyes at my terrible jokes,
Yet we giggle the most, like a pair of blokes.
Your laugh's like a melody, sweet and off-key,
Together we harmonize, just you and me.

We form a tangle, of limbs and of hearts,
Through jumbled adventures, we're never apart.
You spill your coffee, I trip on the rug,
Yet love's in the chaos, we share every hug.

Life's a clumsy waltz, let's dance in the rain,
With twirls and stumbles, we conquer the mundane.
Our moments are funny, our troubles are few,
With you as my partner, I'd never feel blue.

So here's to the laughter and silly delight,
With you in my life, everything's bright.
Entwined in this journey, let's lighten our load,
In the dance of our souls, love's a funny code.

The Heart's Foundation

In our house of giggles, we built a base,
With pancakes on ceilings and love's warm embrace.
Your sock puppet drama makes me laugh till I cry,
As you chase the cat, oh my, oh my!

We stack our dreams on a pile of old shoes,
With laughter as glue, and a dash of our snooze.
Through fumbles and tumbles, we'll build it up right,
Our hearts like a fortress, a comical sight.

The blueprint of silly, with blue skies above,
Our foundation is strong, framed in the stuff of love.
Let's fill it with memories, the laughter and play,
When life throws us curveballs, we'll chuckle away.

So here's to our castle, a folly so grand,
With windows of joy and a backyard of sand.
The heart's silly structure it's crooked yet true,
In this funny old house, it's just me and you.

A Garden of Memories

In a patchwork garden where laughter grows,
We plant seeds of joy where the wild breeze blows.
The daisies are quirky, the roses perplexed,
With thoughts of our past, we're often bemused.

Each flower a story, each stem holds a grin,
From dance-offs in kitchens to ice cream with gin.
Let's water our dreams with a splash of fun,
In this wacky garden, our love is never done.

As we dig through the earth, we unearth the past,
With shovels of humor, our laughs shape a cast.
Up high in the trees, our laughter takes flight,
In a garden of memories, the sun feels just right.

So here's to the blossoms, both silly and sweet,
In the soil of our laughter, we wander, we greet.
With you in this garden, every moment's a thrill,
For in this bouquet of life, my heart's never still.

The Ground Beneath Us

In the garden we can play,
Digging holes just like a sleigh.
With a shovel, I will cheer,
Find a worm and say, "Here, dear!"

When the plants begin to sprout,
I will jump and dance about.
Laughing roots will sway and bend,
A cabbage is my loyal friend.

Raccoons join in with a grin,
Stealing veggies from the bin.
But who can blame them—such a feast!
We'll share it all, to say the least!

Underneath the sun's bright light,
We'll make sure it feels just right.
With laughter echoing all around,
A happier place cannot be found.

Bonds Beyond Time

With my buddy, time's a joke,
We weave moments, laughter's cloak.
Wobbling here, and bouncing there,
In our clocks, we find no care.

When we're lost in memories sweet,
We recall our funny feats.
There's that time I tripped and fell,
You laughed so hard—you rose to yell!

From the dunes to ocean's shore,
Every giggle asks for more.
Life's a dance, both bold and bright,
Twisting together, day and night.

So here's to bonds that last and grow,
Through every ebb and all the flow.
Together, we'll share this ride,
On a laughter-filled, silly tide.

Nature's Embrace

In the trees, the squirrels play,
Mocking humans every day.
With acorns flying through the air,
Nature's jokes are everywhere!

The flowers wear a silly grin,
Dancing when the breezes spin.
Petals tickle charming bees,
In the garden, joy's a breeze!

Mushrooms pop up just to tease,
Whispering, "Hey, try some cheese!"
Every stem has stories to tell,
In this green world, all is well.

So let's frolic, sing, and shout,
Join the fun, there's no doubt.
In this wild, enchanting space,
It's love and laughter we embrace.

Where Souls Intertwine

In a party where souls collide,
We dance together, side by side.
With socks on hands and wigs askew,
We laugh until we're bright and blue!

Each silly word, a jester's charm,
Round and round, there's no alarm.
Twisted tales of love and grace,
In our hearts, there's ample space.

And when the moonlight starts to glow,
We tell ghost stories all aglow.
Haunted laughter fills the room,
We conjure joy, and banish gloom!

In this kaleidoscope of cheer,
Our connections grow sincere.
So let's keep laughing, dancing still,
For in our joy, we find our will.

Anchored in Devotion

In a garden where socks go to hide,
We find the missing pairs side by side.
With laughter as big as a sunflower's grin,
We dance with the weeds, and the weeds let us in.

We argue on pizza, which topping's the best,
While juggling our laundry, we rarely get rest.
Our love's like a trampoline, bouncy and bright,
We jump high together, oh what a delight!

With breakfast in bed that looks like a scene,
Of scrambled confusion, you know what I mean!
Yet even burnt toast can't burn out our spark,
In this kitchen chaos, love leaves a mark.

So here's to our quirks, our moments absurd,
In the tale of our life, love is the bird.
It squawks and it flutters, in sunshine and rain,
Anchored in giggles, we dance through the pain.

Blossom of Togetherness

Two peas in a pod, but one's a bit squished,
In this comedy show, let's not be too dished.
You bring the bananas, I'll bring the bread,
We'll make silly sandwiches, that's how we're fed.

We pick up your socks and then I lose mine,
It's a treasure hunt game—how perfectly divine!
With roots intertwined, like vines in a tangle,
Our love is a jester, with antics to dangle.

We laugh at the table, where dinners go south,
When sauce flies like fireworks straight from our mouth.
Yet even the spills become stories we tell,
In a blossom of silly, we bloom all too well.

So here's to the laughter, the quirks that we share,
In a garden of jokes, let's surely beware.
May our petals stay vibrant, our laughter so free,
In this blossom of ours, you'll always have me.

Threads of Tenderness

We weave our days with a needle of fun,
Stitching up laughter, one by one.
When mischief's afoot, we twirl and we spin,
Knitting odd moments, where do we begin?

The socks that keep disappearing, where do they go?
Under the couch or in the cat's show?
Yet every lost item leads to a giggle,
In the threads of our lives, together we wriggle.

Balancing this life on a tightrope of glee,
With hiccups of chaos, we dance with the tea.
You tell me I'm clumsy, oh what a delight!
But it's in all the stumbles that we take flight.

So here's to the seams that we patch up with grace,
In the tapestry woven, we've found our place.
Each thread tells a story, with laughter to blend,
Together we flourish, there's no end.

Beneath the Canopy of Us

Under our tree, where the squirrels play hide,
We toss our worries, and then they collide.
With branches that tickle and leaves that tease,
In the shade of our joy, we play with the breeze.

The weather may whirl and try to invade,
But we laugh at the storms, let the sun serenade.
Like acorns that tumble from branches so free,
We roll with the punch, oh what a sight to see!

Beneath this grand canopy, our laughter resounds,
As we play silly games, no limits, no bounds.
You slip on a raindrop, I giggle with glee,
In the dance of this life, it's just you and me.

So raise up our voices, let the squirrels know,
We're here with our stories, ready to grow.
In this beautiful chaos, with hearts full and free,
Beneath our great tree, you're the laughter to me.

Nourished by Dreams

In the garden of giggles, we bloom,
Watering laughter to chase away gloom.
With a sprinkle of joy and a dash of cheer,
Every dream planted, we hold it dear.

We dance with the daisies, our circus parade,
In our patch of sunshine, we're never dismayed.
Turnips in tutus, what a sight to behold,
In our silly sanctuary, we grow brave and bold.

With each wacky wish, a seed we set free,
Our hearts like the soil, rich as can be.
Like butterflies in bow ties, we flutter and sway,
Dreams nourished by chuckles, brighten our day.

So here's to the laughter, our sweet serenade,
In this garden of goofy, we've happily played.
With roots in each giggle and branches in fun,
Life's just a joke, and we've already won.

Through Seasons We Stand

Spring brings the blossoms, oh what a sight,
But pollen's a rascal, it gives us a fright.
We sneeze and we giggle, a tickle in nose,
Through all of the seasons, our laughter just grows.

Summer's a sauna, the sun shines too bright,
We dance in the shade, oh what pure delight!
With ice cream mishaps and sunburned tan lines,
We bask in the rays and share all the puns.

Autumn arrives with a crunch underfoot,
We jump into leaves, with our best silly hoot.
Sweaters come out, and we roast all the treats,
Mismatched socks and goofy, are our fashion feats.

Winter brings snowflakes, it's freezing galore,
We build silly snowmen, then tumble and roar.
With cocoa in hand and snowball fights planned,
Through seasons together, in laughter, we stand.

Sown in Trust

Let's plant our hopes in a garden so grand,
With wobbly tomatoes, and corn that can't stand.
We'll water our giggles and sing silly tunes,
As sproutlings of jokes like playful buffoons.

In the soil of absurdity, seeds are so spry,
With dance moves like squirrels, we leap to the sky.
We cultivate courage with every good pun,
With roots of affection, the laughter's begun.

Trusting the sunshine, we skip down the row,
In this playful paradise, our joy starts to grow.
With carrots in capes and beets wearing hats,
We cheer for each other, giggling like cats.

So here's to the garden, we've lovingly turned,
Through love's little whispers, our hearts have all learned.
That friendships are treasures in soil so divine,
Sown in the friendship, forever we'll shine.

Love Like Vines

With tendrils of humor, we intertwine,
Like a grape on a trellis, we sip on the wine.
In the vineyard of laughter, we pluck all the laughs,
Creating our own grape-filled act with no gaffs.

Twisting in circles, we giggle and sway,
In this raucous embrace, where silly holds sway.
Wrapped up in joy, we dance through the night,
With love like grapevines, tangled and bright.

Each leaf tells a story, a jest or a pun,
In the sunshine of friendship, we glitter like fun.
Through harvests of chuckles, the laughter won't cease,
With vines around us, we grow in peace.

So raise up a glass to the bonds that we share,
In the orchard of mirth, we twirl without care.
With roots interwoven, and laughter so fine,
Life's sweetest delight is our love like vines.

Unfurling Together

In the garden, we dance with glee,
Our plants whisper secrets, just you and me.
You prune the roses, I chase the bees,
Fertilizer spills, oh please, oh please!

We grow side by side, a quirky pair,
Your giant sunflowers give me a scare.
I try to tango with wayward vines,
And end up tangled in your bright designs.

With laughter we water our patchy greens,
Mishaps make memories, or so it seems.
We bloom together, our hearts in sync,
We're like a garden filled with pink soda drink.

In this patch of dirt, we've made our space,
With flowers and laughter, we put on a face.
So here's to our garden of giggles and cheer,
Together we flourish, oh how we steer!

The Boughs of Unity

Under the branches, we gather round,
With snacks piled high and laughter abound.
You toss a grape and I take the bait,
And now there's a fruit salad, isn't that great?

Squirrels stare in our comedic delight,
As you trip on roots, it's quite a sight.
We giggle and squabble, like kids on a spree,
Who knew picnic chaos could set us free?

Occluded by branches, the sun runs away,
We argue with shadows, who wins anyway?
Your potato salad, a real culinary art,
Is somehow a sculpture – or is that just heart?

As dusk settles in, and our laughter contends,
We heat up the stories, share jokes like old friends.
Our branches entwined, on this crazy day,
With plates full of joy, we just laugh and play.

Spirit of the Hearth

Around the flames, we roast our dreams,
With marshmallows sticky, or so it seems.
You sing like a bird, off-key in delight,
And I pretend to be your backup tonight.

The fire crackles, a mischief it makes,
Popcorn explodes, oh, what a mistake!
Our laughter echoes, the stars join the fun,
While we dodge rogue sparks, we're always on the run!

The heat from the flames warms more than our toes,
As jokes dance along like those little sparks' shows.
With every silly tale, we build our own lore,
You dance around, saying, "Just one story more!"

So let's keep this spirit alive through the night,
With giggles and s'mores, everything feels right.
In the hearth of our friendship, let passions ignite,
A blaze of our joys, it truly feels bright!

Our Indelible Mark

With crayons and laughter, we scribble our way,
Our masterpieces brightening every gray day.
You draw a cat that looks more like a shoe,
And I swear it's the strangest creature I've ever knew!

We paint outside the lines, a colorful mess,
And giggles erupt at our artistic distress.
The walls get a makeover, not quite divine,
But we'll argue for hours that it's simply sublime.

Each stroke tells a tale, of giggles and dreams,
With markers in hand, we craft our own schemes.
From silly stick figures to wild splashes bright,
Our artwork's a riot, a true delight!

So let's leave our mark, however bizarre,
In the hearts of the ones we adore from afar.
In this gallery of fun, let our laughter soar,
As we color the world, forever more!

Underneath the Stars

Two squirrels danced on the tree,
While rabbits painted with glee.
The moon chuckled above at their craze,
As fireflies twinkled in a vibrant haze.

A cat in a hat played a tune,
Promising dinner by the light of the moon.
But the mice all just shakes their heads,
And planned a wild party instead!

The owl hooted, "Who's in charge?",
With a feathered flair, he looked large.
The chorus of crickets sang loud and clear,
"Let's toast marshmallows and bring on the cheer!"

So here's to the night, so bright and alive,
With friends by your side, it's a surefire drive.
To dance, laugh, and peek at the skies,
In a whimsical world where joy never dies!

Nurtured in Unity

In the meadow, cows wore shades,
Sipping smoothies in cool cascades.
While chickens played hopscotch on the green,
Their clucks creating a fun little scene.

A goat brought cupcakes, stacked up high,
But tripped in delight and sent them awry.
The pigs rolled in laughter, ate up the mess,
While ducks quacked, "You could've impressed!"

The sun stood by, laughing hard,
While everyone waved a fluffy card.
In unity, there's nothing absurd,
Especially when it's warm and blurred!

So if you're feeling a little out of place,
Just join the party, find your space.
With quirky friends, you're never alone,
In this silly barn, you'll find your home!

Sheltered Affection

Beneath the eaves of an old wooden shed,
A cat and a dog shared a cozy bed.
Their dreams intertwined like a silly string,
While the raindrops sang of the warmth they bring.

A wise old turtle joined them, slow,
With tales of adventures in sun and snow.
The cat just yawned, the dog did a snore,
As the turtle recounted his epic explore.

Outside, the rabbits hopped with glee,
Turning rain puddles into a spree.
While the squirrel tried juggling nuts in the air,
And ended up tangled without a care.

Inside the shed, warmth wrapped like a hug,
While outside chaos danced like a bug.
They laughed at the world, so loud and bright,
In their little haven, everything felt right!

Blossoming Bliss

In a garden where daisies wore crowns of cheer,
A gnome broke into dance, oh dear!
While butterflies giggled, flitting about,
Sipping nectar with a sugary spout.

The tulips had a secret, a gossip parade,
Whispering wonders that never would fade.
While the roses blushed, in pink and in red,
Laughing at rabbits who fell out of bed.

Sunshine and laughter bloomed in a patch,
As bees buzzed tunes, a delightful match.
The garden held stories, each petal a song,
In this silly haven, where we all belong.

So here's to the moments, both silly and sweet,
Where joy can be found in each little beat.
Embrace the blossoms that spring from within,
For happiness thrives, where we all begin!

The Essence of Togetherness

In a garden we grow, quite absurd,
With a gnome who's named Fred, quite the word.
He tends to the daisies, a bit too loud,
Singing off-key, drawing quite the crowd.

We share our snacks, like squirrels in spring,
Pantry raids stirring, oh what joy it brings.
Peanut butter dances, on a slice of bread,
While jelly wiggles, with a giggle ahead.

Our potted plant gives us advice each day,
"Water with laughter, not just cliche!"
Its leafy wisdom, can be quite a hoot,
Sharing secrets as we sway to the root.

Together we bloom, in this silly plot,
With perfect imperfections, we've tied the knot.
Our laughter echoes, through the green and the brown,
In this strange little world, we wear the crown.

Heartstrings in Soil

With garden forks in hand, we dig up the past,
Uncovering treasures, a bizarre contrast.
A pair of old shoes, a toy from our youth,
A gnome's sneaky smile, that's the honest truth.

Each weed we pull brings a giggle, you see,
"Look at this dandelion, attempting to flee!"
We play tug-of-war with nature's own grip,
In this tangled love dance, we twirl and we trip.

Beneath the surface, our quirks intertwine,
Like roots in the dirt, in a wobbly line.
We laugh at the mess of our scrapes and our falls,
Each moment a memory, like a garden's calls.

With each passing season, we'll cultivate cheer,
Compiling our moments, year after year.
In this patch of the world, where oddities play,
We'll flourish together, come what may.

Blossoms of Commitment

In the pot of life, we plant seeds of cheer,
With laughter as water, it's crystal clear.
Each sprout is a story, a ridiculously fun,
Like two clowns competing, for the laugh that they've won.

A love that's like soil, just ready to grow,
Through veggies and weeds, we take it slow.
With radishes roguing, and carrots in line,
We munch through the garden, it all tastes divine.

Our planters are mismatched, like socks in a rush,
Yet every odd pairing makes a sweet little hush.
As blossoms of laughter unfold in the sun,
Our garden's a circus, together we run.

In the midst of the chaos, we find our delight,
Two peas in a pod, with our hearts shining bright.
These blossoms of joy, in the light of our days,
Grow stronger together, in the silliest ways.

Flourishing Together

In a quirky patch where odd plants abound,
We tackle the world, goin' rounds and rounds.
Our veggies debate, like old pals who jest,
Tomorrow's salad, we'll put to the test.

The sun's our cheerleader, the rain brings a song,
In this wondrous chaos, we truly belong.
A tomato with swagger, an eggplant that twirls,
This garden's a stage, our laughter unfurls.

Through storms and through sunshine, we frolic and play,
A routine of silliness brightens our day.
With roots interwoven through mischief and glee,
Every joke over dinner, undeniably free.

So here's to our patch, where absurdity thrives,
With love as the fertilizer, our spirit survives.
In this garden of nonsense, we find our best light,
Together we flourish, through day and through night.

The Oasis of Togetherness

In a desert of socks, we find our pairs,
Giggling at chaos, as love declares.
With mismatched shoes, we dance around,
In this sandy spot, joy is found.

Cacti hug tightly, ensuring we share,
A garden of laughter, beyond compare.
Watering plants with our silly dreams,
In this oasis, everything gleams.

We swap our stories with playful bites,
Grapes thrown sky-high reach new heights.
In this sandy retreat, there's never a frown,
Together we thrive, no need to drown.

So let's toast with juice, be sure it's not hot,
In this sunny patch, we forget all we've got.
For in this desert, we're never alone,
Our oasis of quirks is the best way to roam.

Soil of the Heart

In the garden of giggles, we plant our seeds,
With laughter as fertilizer, we grow what we need.
Roots intertwine in a comical dance,
In our patch of craziness, we take every chance.

We sprinkle our cares with a generous hand,
Weeds of doubt vanish, here we stand.
A bouquet of silliness blooms every day,
In this heart-soil, we chuckle and play.

Each morning we water with hugs from the heart,
Tending this plot, we all play a part.
Though sometimes we trip on the garden hose,
Together we laugh at the way that it goes.

Through rain or through shine, we plant and we grow,
The soil is our love, let's revel in the flow.
With cow manure jokes, we dig deep and thrice,
In this comedic earth, everything's nice.

Harmony in Diversity

In a patchwork quilt, we stitch our fate,
Colors and patterns—oh! Isn't it great?
A pineapple and a pickle make quite a pair,
A fruit salad band in the wide-open air.

With every odd couple, we harmonize well,
Mixing our quirks, there's magic to tell.
A rhythm of laughter, a beat so delight,
We celebrate differences day and night.

From tacos to sushi, it's all on the plate,
Creating a banquet that's simply first-rate.
Each flavor brings laughter, a joyous refrain,
Diverse like our tastes, let's dance in the rain.

So come one, come all, bring your odd shoes,
In this fun orchestra, there's nothing to lose.
Together we build, with whimsy and glee,
A garden of voices that sings, "Just be free!"

A Landscape of Love

In the rolling hills of our silly delight,
Where clouds throw confetti and dreams take flight.
We skip through the meadows with giggles so loud,
Chasing our shadows, oh, aren't we proud?

The trees laugh and chuckle at all of our pranks,
While rivers of joy offer us thanks.
With daisies as helmets, we march on a spree,
Each footstep a dance, oh, can't you see?

Sometimes we tumble, then rise with a grin,
Finding the mirth that was always within.
The mountains are puns, the valleys are games,
In this vibrant space, we escape all the names.

So grab a good friend and whirl on the grass,
In this joyful panorama, let worries all pass.
With a landscape of laughter, we find our way,
Together forever, come what may!

Nurtured by the Sun

In a garden of laughter, we sprout,
Chasing butterflies, while dancing about.
Our jokes bloom bright, like flowers in May,
Who knew love could grow in such a silly way?

We plant our dreams, a plucky surprise,
Watering giggles, under sunny skies.
With every raindrop, a new pun will rise,
Like daisies popping up, oh how time flies!

Sunshine embraces us, not just for show,
We roll in the grass, let our friendship grow.
A cabbage of warmth, no need for a frown,
We're the silliest veggies in this love town!

So let's laugh together, like roots intertwined,
In this wacky garden, true joy we will find.
With petals of humor, we bloom ever bright,
Under the sun, oh what a delight!

Seeds of Connection

We're two little seeds in a big, goofy plot,
Sprinkled with laughter, connecting the dot.
You plant the punchlines; I'll water the wit,
Together we flourish, I'm glad we commit!

As we sprout into stories that make flowers smile,
We wiggle in joy, in our own silly style.
A cactus may poke, but we've got our charm,
With humor as fertilizer, we're safe from harm!

Through laughter, we travel, across fields so grand,
Creating a forest of joy, hand in hand.
When friends come together, the sprouts all agree,
Life's a hilarious garden, so wild and free!

Among the wild weeds, we stand tall and proud,
With quirks and laughs, we're a jolly crowd.
So let's plant our hearts, let the good times roll,
In this garden of friendship, we're on a stroll!

Ties of the Heart

Like vines all twisted in a joyous embrace,
We stumble and tumble, but we love this race.
With a chuckle or two, our roots are aligned,
Tangled up in laughter, we'll never unwind!

Our friendship's a patchwork, sewn with a grin,
With patches of humor, where every joke wins.
We bind up the sillies with twine made of cheer,
In this garden of giggles, we've nothing to fear!

As sprinkled confetti leads us on our way,
We're giddy as flowers that sway and play.
When storms try to rattle our silly old ties,
We dance in the downpour, that's how love flies!

So here's to the bonds that can bloom in the night,
With laughter we scatter, in beams of pure light.
In this fantastic garden, we'll flourish as one,
With wit as our water, and smiles like the sun!

Beneath One Sky

Under the same roof, we share all our dreams,
Cracking up loud, so silly it seems.
With tickles and twirls, we brighten the day,
As clouds of mischief keep troubles at bay!

No storm can divide us, we weather each joke,
Laughing like sprouts when the sunlight they soak.
We're twinkling like stars in our playful delight,
Beneath the same sky, everything feels right!

With goofy ambitions, we reach for the high,
Creating new waves, like a kite in the sky.
We flip and we flail, in our own little way,
Life's a comedy show, come join us and play!

So let's cherish these moments, grow stronger each day,
In this vivid adventure, we'll giggle and sway.
Under one sky, we'll share joy and glee,
For love is the laughter that sets our hearts free!

www.ingramcontent.com/pod-product-compliance
Lightning Source LLC
Chambersburg PA
CBHW070325120526
44590CB00017B/2817